Pebble® Plus

ICE AGE ANIMALS

Dodos

by Melissa Higgins

Consulting Editor: Gail Saunders-Smith, PhD

Content Consultant: Margaret M. Yacobucci, PhD
Education and Outreach Coordinator,
Paleontological Society; Associate Professor,
Department of Geology, Bowling Green State University

Raintree is an imprint of Capstone Global Library Limited, a company incorporated in England and Wales
having its registered office at 7 Pilgrim Street, London, EC4V 6LB – Registered company number: 6695582

www.raintree.co.uk
myorders@raintree.co.uk

Editorial Credits
Jeni Wittrock, editor; Peggie Carley and Janet Kusmierski, designers; Wanda Winch, media researcher; Laura
Manthe, production specialist

ISBN 978 1 4062 9365 4 (hardback)
18 17 16 15 14
10 9 8 7 6 5 4 3 2 1

ISBN 978 1 4062 9372 2 (paperback)
19 18 17 16
10 9 8 7 6 5 4 3 2 1

British Library Cataloguing in Publication Data
A full catalogue record for this book is available from the British Library.

Photo Credits
Illustrator: Jon Hughes
Shutterstock: Alex Staroseltsev, snowball, April Cat, icicles, Konstanttin,
cover background, Leigh Prather, ice crystals, pcruciatti, interior background

Every effort has been made to contact copyright holders of material reproduced in this book. Any omissions
will be rectified in subsequent printings if notice is given to the publisher.

All the Internet addresses (URLs) given in this book were valid at the time of going to press. However, due to
the dynamic nature of the Internet, some addresses may have changed, or sites may have changed or ceased
to exist since publication. While the author and publisher regret any inconvenience this may cause readers, no
responsibility for any such changes can be accepted by either the author or the publisher.

Printed and bound in China.

Contents

Flightless

A bird the size of a turkey walks through the forest. A sudden noise sends other birds into flight. But not the dodo. This bird cannot fly.

Dodos lived only on the island of Mauritius. This small island in the Indian Ocean had no predators. Safe on their island, dodos did not need to fly.

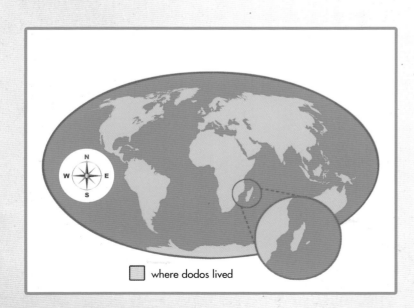

where dodos lived

Made for walking

Over millions of years,

dodos' wings became small.

Dodos were too heavy to fly.

Instead they travelled on

their yellow legs.

Blue-grey feathers covered dodos' bodies. They had long, strong beaks. The dodo's closest living relatives are pigeons.

Life on the ground

Dodos lived their entire lives
on the forest floor. They ate
fallen fruits and nuts.
They may have also eaten fish.

Dodos made nests on the ground. Females laid a single egg. Dodos were watchful mothers.

Dodo's end

Dodos lived through the last Ice Age. Earth was cooler then, but ice and snow never reached Mauritius.

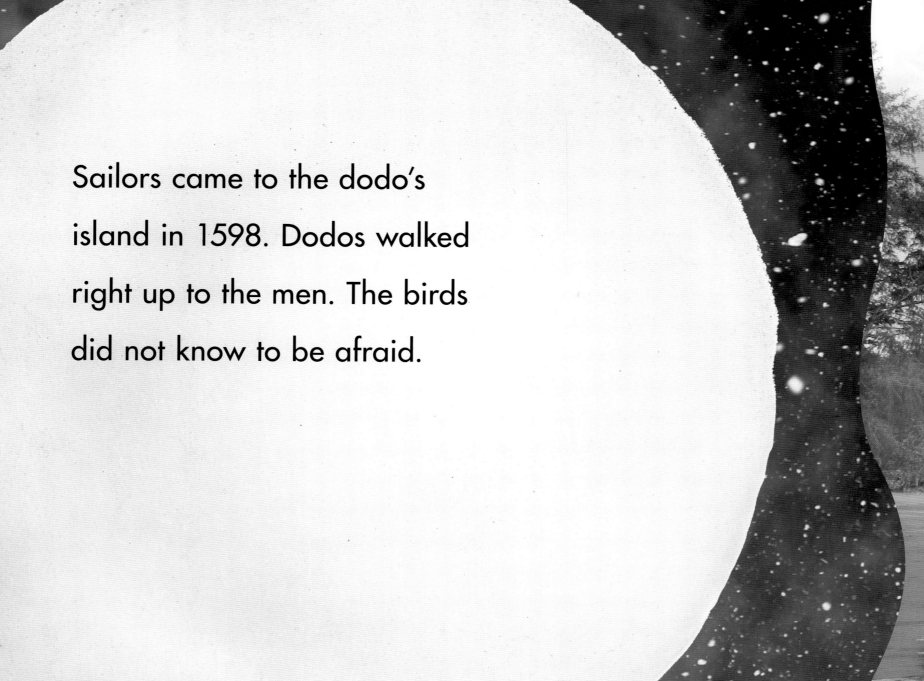

Sailors came to the dodo's
island in 1598. Dodos walked
right up to the men. The birds
did not know to be afraid.

Sailors ate dodos for food. The sailors' dogs and cats hunted dodos and their eggs. By 1693 the dodos had become extinct.

Glossary

beak hard front part of the mouth of birds and some dinosaurs; also called a bill

extinct no longer living; an extinct animal is one that has died out, with no more of its kind

Ice Age time when much of Earth was covered in ice; the last ice age ended about 11,500 years ago

predator animal that hunts other animals for food

relative part of the same family

sailor person who works on a boat

Read more

Brilliant Birds (Extreme Animals), Isabel Thomas
(Raintree, 2013)

The Ice Age Tracker's Guide, Adrian Lister and
Martin Ursell (Frances Lincoln Children's Books, 2010)

Dinosaurs (First Facts), Charlie Gardner
(Dorling Kindersley, 2012)

Websites

www.museumofmystery.org.uk
Solve another extinction mystery and find out what
happened to dinosaurs.

www.nhm.ac.kids-only/dinosaurs/
Find out everything you need to know about prehistoric
life. Look at 3-D dinosaurs, learn fun facts, play games
and take a quiz!

Index